MARKETING

MARKETING

BRIAN TRACY

AMACOM AMERICAN MANAGEMENT ASSOCIATION
New York · Atlanta · Brussels · Chicago · Mexico City
San Francisco · Shanghai · Tokyo · Toronto · Washington, D.C.

This publication is designed to provide accurate and authoritative information in regard to the subject matter covered. It is sold with the understanding that the publisher is not engaged in rendering legal, accounting, or other professional service. If legal advice or other expert assistance is required, the services of a competent professional person should be sought.

Library of Congress Cataloging-in-Publication Data has been applied for and is on file.

About AMA

American Management Association (www.amanet.org) is a world leader in talent development, advancing the skills of individuals to drive business success. Our mission is to support the goals of individuals and organizations through a complete range of products and services, including classroom and virtual seminars, webcasts, webinars, podcasts, conferences, corporate and government solutions, business books, and research. AMA's approach to improving performance combines experiential learning—learning through doing—with opportunities for ongoing professional growth at every step of one's career journey.

Printing number
19 20 PC/LSCC 10 9 8 7 6 5

CONTENTS

Introduction

THE PRIMARY reason for the success or failure of a business is determined by the success or failure of the marketing effort. According to Dun & Bradstreet, 48 percent of all business failures can be attributed to a slowing down or ineffectiveness in the area of marketing and sales. In our dynamic, competitive economy, marketing is the core function of every successful enterprise. No matter what business you are in, you are in the "marketing business."

In this powerful, practical book on marketing, you will learn or relearn twenty-one key ideas, and many "subideas," that you can use to improve your strategic marketing results—starting immediately.

Strategic marketing is the art and science of determining what your customers and future customers really want and need—and can use and afford—and then helping them to get it by creating and structuring your products and services in such a way that they satisfy the specific needs of the customers you have identified.

The goal of strategic marketing is to enable you to sell more of your offerings at higher prices over an extended geographical area and achieve market stability, strength, and leadership.

Rule Number One

The starting point of successful marketing is for you to remember that customers are always right. They buy for their reasons, not yours. Customers are selfish, demanding, ruthless, disloyal, and fickle. But they are always right, based on their own needs, wants, desires, and ways of thinking. Customers will change suppliers whenever they perceive that they will be better served elsewhere.

Your ability to appeal to their real desires, and to satisfy their wants and needs as they perceive them, will largely determine your success in business.

Marketing is a skill set that can and must be learned by keeping certain ideas and concepts in mind continually, and by asking certain vital questions regularly. If you take the time to think through the answers to the questions in this book, you will sharpen your marketing skills considerably.

The most important part of this book is what you do afterward. It is the specific actions that you take, and how quickly you take those actions, that will determine the entire value of this book for you.

When you read or think of an action you can take to improve your marketing, act on it immediately. Don't delay. Develop a sense of urgency and a bias for action. These are the essential qualities of all great businesspeople.

ONE

The Purpose of a Business

MANY PEOPLE think that the purpose of a business is simply to make a profit. The real purpose, however, as Peter Drucker explained, is to "create and keep a customer." All the efforts of a successful business are aimed at creating customers in some way. Profits are the result of creating and keeping customers in a cost-effective way over time.

The cost of creating customers initially is very high. The cost of keeping them is far lower than the cost of creating them in the first place. If you study the companies that are the most efficient at marketing, you will find that their strategies are all aimed at creating customers and then holding on to them.

Quality as a Marketing Strategy

Perhaps the most profitable marketing strategy is that of developing your products or services to a high level of quality. Quality is the most powerful and effective of all marketing strategies. Fully 90 percent of your business success will be determined by the quality of what you produce in the first place. People will always buy from a quality supplier, pay higher prices, and return over and over again to a company that provides them with high-quality goods and services.

What is quality? This subject has been discussed and debated for years. Philip Crosby, founder of the Quality College, said that "quality is the degree to which your product does what you say it will do when you sell it, and continues to do it."

Perhaps the best definition of a *brand*, which is your reputation in the marketplace, is "the promises you make and the promises you keep." Your quality rating is determined by what percentage of the time your product or service delivers on the promises you made to attract your customer to buy in the first place.

The second fundamental strategy for successful marketing is quality service. According to PIMS (Profit Impact for Marketing Strategy), a study conducted over many years by Harvard University, the quality of a product is contained in two factors: the product itself, and the way the product is sold and serviced.

It is not only the product itself, but the way that you treat your customers, from the first contact through their entire time with you using your product or service. People will always come back to a quality supplier of goods and services, no matter what the price.

How They Feel About You

There is another critical factor in marketing success, and it has to do with relationships. More and more today we are finding that it is the quality of our business relationships that determines whether we create and keep a substantial number of customers.

Sometimes I ask my audiences, "What percentage of people's decision making is emotional and what percentage is logical?"

After they have thrown out a few answers, I tell them, "People are 100 percent emotional." They decide emotionally, and then they justify logically. It is how they feel, and especially how they believe they will feel after the purchase, that determines whether they make the purchase at all.

Jan Carlzon, the former president of SAS Airlines who made SAS one of the most profitable companies in Europe, wrote a book about his experiences called *Moments of Truth*. In this groundbreaking book, he pointed out that every customer contact is a "moment of truth" that has an effect and can largely determine whether or not that customer ever does business with you again. Since the cost of satisfying an existing customer is about one-tenth of the cost of marketing, advertising, promoting, and selling to a new customer, it is the companies that can create and keep customers by taking excellent care of them that are invariably the most profitable and fastest growing.

Buying Customers

Each company is in the business of "buying customers." All companies have a specific "cost of acquisition," whether they know what it is or not. This is perhaps the single most important cost factor in the success of any business.

Your cost of acquisition is composed of all the monies that you pay to any person, and in any way, to buy a customer for the first time. A company stays in business if it can buy customers at a lower amount than the net profit that the customer will yield to the company in the course of the customer's buying lifetime.

Whenever you read about companies that have sales in the millions or even billions of dollars, but still lose money, you are seeing an example of the old saying: "We lose money on every sale, but we hope to make it up on the volume."

When companies lose money, it is primarily because the cost of acquisition to that company for an individual customer is greater than the total profit that the customer will yield to the company.

If your company can buy customers at a lower cost than the profit you can earn from that customer, you can spend almost any amount to buy more and more customers. This is one of the great secrets of business success, and it is a core requirement for effective marketing.

Four Approaches to Successful Marketing

THERE ARE four ways that you can approach your market with your products and services.

Creating Utility

The first is by creating *utility*, usefulness, and by satisfying the needs of your customers to achieve a specific result. This approach requires that you offer customers something they need and can use to accomplish their other goals. A perfect example is a shovel or a truck, each of which has utility value, but maybe not the end that the customer has in mind. You've heard it said that "people don't buy drills; they buy quarter-inch holes."

An example of a new industry that was built on utility value or needs is FedEx. Years before Apple created entirely new industries for the iPod, iPhone, and iPad, FedEx created an industry for overnight mail that never existed before. Fred Smith, the founder of FedEx, saw an immense need for rapid letter and package delivery overnight because of the slowness of regular mail.

Look at your market today. What will your customers and potential customers want, need, and be willing to pay for in the months and years ahead? As Peter Drucker said, "The trends are everything." What are the trends in customer demands in your market? If you can answer this question accurately, you can often leapfrog over your competition and dominate a new market even before it emerges.

Pricing Properly

A second approach to marketing is by changing your pricing. By bringing your goods and services into the price range of your customers, you can open up entirely new markets that do not today exist. Henry Ford became one of the richest men in the world, after struggling financially for decades, because he had this rare insight. He saw that by mass producing the automobile, he could get the price down to the point where most Americans would be able to afford one. In achieving this goal, he revolutionized manufacturing and mass consumption forever.

Many companies have been able to achieve market leadership by focusing on bringing their prices into the affordability range of more customers. What we have found is that the greater your market share, and the lower your cost of production, the lower the price that you can charge. The Japanese use this strategy brilliantly year after year. First of all, they price their products and services as low as possible to gain market share. As they gain market share, they begin to enjoy economies of scale, manufacturing their products at ever-lower prices. They then pass the savings on to their customers with even lower prices and increase their market share once more. Eventually, they end up dominating many of the markets they have entered.

Your Customer's Reality

The third strategy in marketing is adapting to the customer's reality, both social and economic. A perfect example is how Sears became the world's largest retailer of its time by initiating an unconditional money-back guarantee policy in the catalog business.

The customer's reality up until that time was that if they bought something that didn't work or didn't fit, they were stuck with it. Sears realized that the way to overcome that major barrier to purchasing was to adapt their product offering to the customer's reality, which led to a revolution in merchandising and retail sales.

Every product offers a "key benefit" that is the primary reason the customer would buy that product. Each product or service also triggers a "key fear," which is what holds the customer back from buying the product or service in the first place. For example, customers are terrified of risk. They are afraid of paying too much, getting the wrong product, losing their money, and getting stuck with something that is inappropriate for their purposes. Whatever their fear is, it is the main reason that qualified prospects hold back from buying any product or service, at any price.

When you can emphasize the key benefit, the unique added value that a customer will receive by buying your product or service, and at the same time take away his or her major fear, you can open up an enormous market for what you sell.

Delivering True Value

The fourth approach to marketing strategy is for you to deliver what represents "true value" to the customer. True value can only be identified by working closely with your customers.

IBM is the perfect example. The company controlled 80 percent of the world computer market in its heyday, and for good reason. IBM discovered that in the field of high-tech and high-end equipment that sells for hundreds of thousands or millions of dollars, it was not the functionality of the computer that attracted buyers as much as it was the assurance the computer would be serviced and repaired quickly if something went wrong. IBM provided not only world-class computer products, but also the security that once you bought from IBM, you were protected with perhaps the best service support in the world if the equipment broke down for any reason. This was "true value."

Three Key Questions in Marketing

THERE ARE three key questions to ask with regard to marketing, especially with a new product or idea. Often, if your sales are not satisfactory for any reason with an existing product, you can ask these three questions. Most companies ask question number one, but it is astonishing how many companies that I consult for have never asked the other questions.

Does a Market Exist?

The first question is: "Is there a market?" Are there people out there who will actually buy the product or service that you're thinking about bringing to the market? Remember that the basic success/failure ratio in new products is 80/20. That is, 80 percent of all new products will fail. They will not achieve significant market share and the company will lose money and sometimes go out of business.

Twenty percent of new products will succeed in that they will pay their costs of investment and turn a profit. One of these twenty will be a star. Of 100 new products that are introduced to the market in any given year, only one is going to be a runaway bestseller. Think, for example, about the market for new applications for smartphones.

MARKET RESEARCH

In 2012, U.S. companies spent more than $8 billion on market research of all kinds. The primary reason companies buy market research is to discover whether or not there's a market for a new product or service idea, who or what constitutes that market, and what the product or service would have to do to be sold at a price that would yield a sufficient profit. And even with all this market research, fully 80 percent of new products and services fail within the first year or two.

Today, there is a better strategy. And it is to "get a customer first." Whenever you have a new product or service idea, immediately call a customer in person (no surveys, questionnaires, or focus groups) and tell this customer that you have this new product or service idea. Would he or she buy it? How much would the customer pay for it? What flaws or weaknesses does the customer see in your initial idea for a new product or service?

By doing early market testing, and by asking your customers for their candid opinions, you can drastically speed up "time to market" and reduce your costs of new product development at the same time.

What Is the Size of the Market?

The second question you need to ask is whether the market for your product or service is *large enough*. This is a question that, surprisingly enough, people don't ask and answer. Yet you need to know: Can you sell enough of your product or service to make it economically worthwhile?

In your initial analysis, you determine exactly how much it will cost to produce your product or service, and the price that you will have to achieve in order to make the product or service profitable, especially in comparison with other ways you can spend that same amount of money.

You then determine how many units of your product you will have to sell in a week, a month, and a year to make this a worthwhile investment of your time and trouble. Finally, you determine if there are enough potential customers out there who will buy your product or service in the time span you have predicted.

Is the Market Concentrated?

The third question to ask is: "Is the market concentrated enough?" Just because you can find people in different places who say they would buy your product or service, that's no assurance that the market is concentrated enough that you can reach it with existing advertising methods and existing market channels.

You may find that there is a market for 100,000 units of a new product or service, but it is spread out all over North America in 10,000 cities, towns, and villages. How are you going to reach that market in a cost-effective way? Remember, you are in the business of buying customers. Once you have a product that people will buy, your cost of acquisition will be the critical factor determining your success or failure,

A product or service for which there is a large market may not be feasible for you simply because you cannot promote to that market with existing advertising media or through existing market channels. The good news today is that it is possible for you to reach vastly more specialized markets in small areas with the Internet, and at lower prices than ever before.

It has been said that the Internet is the best and *worst* of all marketing tools. It is the worst because the majority of people that you approach will have no interest and will probably delete your message upon receipt. It is the *best* because you can reach hundreds of thousands and even millions of prospective customers at a very low cost, enabling you to find the proverbial "needle in the haystack."

FOUR

Market Research and Market Intelligence

THERE ARE many parallels between marketing strategy and military strategy. The objective of both strategies is to win, in the marketplace and on the battlefield. All successful military campaigns are based on excellent intelligence and knowledge of the enemy. All successful marketing campaigns are based on good research and good market intelligence: knowing what your competitors are doing and what else is going on in the marketplace.

Remember, you are not Steve Jobs. It is never a good idea to rely on your own feelings or opinions about what customers will buy or not buy. You need to subject your thoughts, feelings, and ideas to the cold, harsh reality of market research and the opinions of other people.

Ask for Their Opinion

Market research can be done in a variety of effective, inexpensive ways today. Probably your first line of attack should be a customer survey via Internet. Our favorite is Survey Monkey.com, a free service that allows you to put together a series of questions to survey a large population quickly and get fast and accurate answers to your marketing questions. You can build your mailing list with your customers' names and those of your noncustomers from the past.

Another way to do market research, as I mentioned in the previous chapter, is to telephone directly some of your best customers, your "sweetheart customers," and ask them for their opinions and advice on this new product idea of yours. Perhaps you can bring some of them together for lunch or even for a meeting after dinner. Their candid comments and observations can be invaluable to you.

Another way to do market research, one of the oldest and most popular, is to use a focus group. Bring in a group of your customers or potential customers, sit them around a table, and ask as many questions as you possibly can about what they think of your new product or service idea. They will tell you about your strengths and weaknesses, and what they think of your pricing, your packaging, and almost every other factor that you ask them about—including your competitors.

Four Questions

Successful market research is based on careful analysis and accurate answers to the right questions. There are four important questions, described here, that you need to cover.

WHO IS YOUR CUSTOMER?

Who buys your product now? Who bought it in the past? Who is likely to buy it in the future? What are their ages, education level, income, current tastes or consumption patterns, occupations, family structure, and so on? These are your customer *demographics*, the observable factors of a customer, and they are the starting point of all market research.

You also need to know the *psychographics* of your customers. These are their thoughts, feelings, values, attitudes, desires, needs, hopes, dreams, ambitions, and aspirations.

WHERE IS YOUR CUSTOMER?

Geography is especially important in determining when and how you are going to market your product or service. Is your customer primarily urban or rural, located in wealthy neighborhoods or in middle-class areas?

The first cookie store Debbi Fields opened was a failure. Because of her ignorance of retail marketing, she located it on a side street a few steps away from the main concourse where people were going past. As a result, no one walked past her store, and she sold very few cookies.

When she opened her second Mrs. Fields store, she paid higher rent but she was located on a main sidewalk, where people regularly walked back and forth in front of the store and couldn't miss seeing her cookies displayed in the glass case. The rest is history. Before the dust had settled, Debbi Fields had built more than 300 stores and created a $500 million fortune.

HOW DOES YOUR CUSTOMER BUY?

This third question explores whether your customer normally purchases your product through direct mail, wholesale, retail, or online.

Napoleon Hill once wrote, "Never attempt to violate human nature and win." What he meant was that people are creatures of habit. They are accustomed to buying things in a certain way. It may take a long time, if ever, for them to become used to buying a product or service in a different way from the way they now know.

Of course, there are massive exceptions. Think Amazon. Busy men and women with work and family responsibilities can get a product or service faster by ordering it from Amazon than they actually could by going out to a store and shopping for the product or service in their spare time, of which they have less and less.

WHAT DOES IT DO?

The final question is: "What is the product being used or bought for?" What do your customers intend to do with the product or service once they purchase it? Customers do not buy products or services themselves. They buy the benefit, change, improvement, or outcome that they anticipate enjoying as a result of making the purchase decision. You must be crystal clear about how and why your customers will be better off buying and using your product or service than they would be if they did not buy it from you, or if they bought it from a competitor.

A Simple Discovery

In my business career, I have had all kinds of experiences in market research. One good example was when we began importing Suzuki four-wheel-drive vehicles from Japan. We set up sixty-five dealerships across western Canada and experienced a variety of sales results, some excellent and some quite poor.

We hired a market research firm to do some "quick and dirty" research to find out who was buying our vehicles and where we were getting the highest sales.

The firm telephoned several hundreds of our purchasers and found, to no one's surprise, that the people who were buying these off-road-capable vehicles were people who lived near mountains and other areas where four-wheel drives were very useful. People who lived in flat areas and in cities where four-wheel-drive vehicles were of little value were not very good potential customers.

Once we had this research, the results seemed quite logical to us. But until we did the research, we didn't realize how important it was. As a result of these findings, we changed our advertising budgets, our promotional activities, and our vehicle allocations to dealers. Our sales went through the roof. We stopped trying to sell to people who were not good potential customers and focused all of our efforts on people who were the most likely to buy the fastest.

FIVE

Customer-Focused Marketing

SUCCESSFUL marketing places the customer at the center of all planning and decision making. Everybody in the company is focused on the customer at all times. The company develops an obsession with customer service. Employees communicate, interact, and stay close to their customers. Continual customer contact and market research are essential to ongoing customer satisfaction.

When Buck Rodgers was the president of U.S. operations at IBM, he emphasized that every single person in the corporation must look upon himself as a customer service representative. Your company will be successful to the degree to which each person in your company thinks about the customers all the time. This even includes the people who sweep the floors, drive the trucks, or answer the telephones.

Own the Problem

My favorite example of this attitude was when I was conducting seminars for IBM and I had failed to find out where the seminar was being held the following day. I phoned from the West Coast to the East Coast after regular business hours to see if I could get an answer. When a man answered the phone at the IBM offices, I explained my dilemma, and he told me that he would get back to me with an answer as soon as possible.

Within fifteen minutes he called back and told me that he had contacted the seminar organizer and found out the name and address of the hotel where I needed to be the next day after my cross-country flight. I thanked him and then said, "I know I'm calling you after hours. You must be working late tonight." He replied, "Of course I'm working late. I am the janitor."

I told him I appreciated his help very much and asked how he was able to get me this information. He replied with those wonderful words, "Here at IBM, whoever answers the phone owns the problem."

Think About Your Customer

There is a metaphysical law of concentration that says, "Whatever you dwell upon, grows." This means that whatever you think about and reflect upon continually, grows and increases in your reality.

When you focus on customer satisfaction, on making your customers happy in every way possible, you continually discover new and better ways to achieve this goal. What is your company philosophy? Are you determined to satisfy your customers to the utmost and in the best way possible?

When you think about your customers all the time, your customers will then think about you. When you make your customers the central focus of your attention, you will discover faster, better, cheaper, and easier ways to satisfy them, and they will reward you by coming back over and over again.

Restaurant Service

One of my favorite seafood restaurants is a national chain called Truluck's. From my first visit to a Truluck's restaurant (and I have since visited many of these restaurants in different parts of the country), I noticed a feature that is often not experienced in other restaurants. The service was absolutely *excellent*. Every single person in the company, from the person who answered the phone to accept my reservation all the way through to the busboy who removed dishes and filled water glasses, was absolutely wonderful in terms of customer service.

When I asked the manager of one Truluck's about my perception, he smiled a bit guiltily and told me that service is the central focus and obsession of everyone in the company, from the president all the way down to the dishwasher in the kitchen. The restaurant owners had come to the conclusion early on that there would always be other seafood restaurants, and even other expensive seafood restaurants, so they could not simply compete on the basis of the food.

They had to compete on the basis of something that connected with customers emotionally, and that was the warmth and effusiveness of the customer service.

Your Quality Service Strategy

In Chapter 1, I talked about developing a quality service strategy for your business. How could you make your customer service faster, more efficient, warmer, and more customer focused than your competitors? Often, this can be the one factor that gives you a competitive edge in your marketplace.

When you identify your target market and your ideal or perfect customer, the very customer that you want most to attract and to buy from you, you may need to change your positioning so that you appeal to exactly that customer. In what ways are your very best customers different from other people, and what appeals could you develop for those customers that you want most to attract and keep?

SIX

Why People Buy

PEOPLE BUY products and services to satisfy their needs. In economics, they say that every action that you or I take is because of what is called a "felt dissatisfaction." We feel dissatisfied in our current condition for some reason. Because of this dissatisfaction, we are internally motivated or driven to take an action of some kind to relieve this dissatisfaction. Think of the example of sitting on a pin. The discomfort triggers immediate action to relieve the pain and to achieve a state of greater satisfaction, which does not involve the pin.

The ABC Model
There is an ABC principle of human motivation. In this case, the letters stand for Antecedents, Behaviors, and Consequences.

The *antecedents* represent about 15 percent of the motivation to buy a product, or to act in any way. The antecedents are composed of previous experiences, thoughts, feelings, and other factors.

The *consequences* represent 85 percent of the motivation to make an act or to buy a product or service.

The middle letter *B* refers to the *behaviors* that are necessary to move from antecedents to consequences.

In this simple model, the antecedents are the felt dissatisfaction, either real or triggered by advertising and promotion. The consequences are the state of greater satisfaction or pleasure that the customer anticipates enjoying by buying and using your product or service. The behavior is the action that the customer must take to move from A to C.

Clarity Is Essential

One of the reasons for passivity, paralysis, or the failure to take action to buy your product, regardless of your advertising or promotional activities, is that your potential customers do not see or understand how they will be better off by buying your product or service. Even more, your prospect does not see how he will be so *much better off* that he can justify the cost, expense, and trouble of moving from his current state to the supposedly better state that your product or service offers.

People always buy products and services to improve their conditions in some way—to achieve a state of greater satisfaction. People won't buy a product or service unless they feel that they will get an improvement that more than justifies the cost and trouble of making the purchase in the first place. Focusing your marketing efforts on how your prospective customer is going to be better off is the key to success in advertising and promotion.

The Problem to Be Solved

People buy *solutions* to their problems. Always think in terms of the "problem to be solved." What is the problem that your product or service will solve for your prospective customer?

People buy the satisfaction of their *needs*. What is the "need to be satisfied" that your product or service can offer your prospective customer?

People buy to achieve their *goals*. What is the goal that your product or service will help your customer to achieve, and which is important enough to the customer that she will pay money, time, and trouble to acquire it?

People buy because they have a *pain* that your product or service will take away. What is the pain that your product or service resolves for your customer?

How Will They Feel?

One of the most important discoveries to come out of the Harvard research by Theodore Levitt is that people buy the *feeling* that they anticipate enjoying as a result of purchasing and using your product or service. What is the exact feeling that your customers will enjoy when they buy what you sell?

It is not the product or service itself; it is always the emotion that your product or service triggers or stimulates.

People buy for *psychic* satisfaction—that is, emotional reasons—far more than they buy for any other reason. What is the most important emotion that people will enjoy as a result of buying and using your product or service?

This is why quality, service, and especially relationships are so important. They generate the emotional component of any product or service in the mind of the customer. They generate the feelings of security, comfort, status, prestige, warmth, and personal connection. What exactly does your customer anticipate feeling when thinking of purchasing your product or service? How could you tailor your marketing efforts to trigger this emotion in your ideal customers?

Save or Gain Time or Money
People in business buy products and services to save or gain time or money. Time and money are almost interchangeable in terms of business results. Every appeal aimed at saving time or money, or gaining time or money, is a strong emotional motivator to people in business who are dependent for their success and security on personal and financial results.

Desire for Gain, Fear of Loss
There are two basic motivations that underlie all action: the desire for gain and the fear of loss. How does your product or service appeal to these needs? How does your product or service help customers to gain something that they want, or to avoid losing something that they value?

The more basic the need that the customer has, the more simple and direct will be the appeal that gets results. Survival and security needs are the most powerful motivators. People want to survive and be secure and are strongly motivated to take whatever steps necessary to avoid losing safety and security. If you are appealing to a security need, such as a home security system with a smoke alarm, then your appeal can be quite basic, something like, "Don't let your family die in the night. Provide the necessary security." This message strikes straight to the heart of the matter and triggers the desire on the part of the prospect to take a buying action of some kind.

If what you are selling is a complex or indirect need, like perfume or jewelry, then your market approach has to be much more subtle. Perhaps the most famous advertisement for perfume was the billboard and full-page magazine ads starring Catherine Deneuve, where she appears next to a bottle of Chanel No. 5, saying, "You're worth it."

Think Out of the Box

When Steve Jobs came back in to Apple in 1996, the company was almost broke. He recognized that they could not grow the company selling the same products they had been marketing for more than twenty years. They needed a breakthrough product that would open up an entirely new market for them. Steve Jobs eventually settled on what became known as the iPod.

Producing the iPod required completely new technology, and advances on old technology, but it also required completely reshaping the entire market of selling and delivering songs to play on a pocket device.

After developing the product, negotiating single-song purchase contracts with most of the big record companies, setting up the iTunes online store, and preparing to go to market, Apple was still struggling for a simple advertising slogan that would summarize the iPod's benefits for people who had never seen or used such a product before. It finally came up with the breakthrough slogan, "1,000 songs in your pocket." The rest is history. Apple sold 50 million iPods at 50 percent profit. This product started Apple on its rise to becoming the most valuable company in the world.

What is the "1,000 songs in your pocket" slogan that you could develop for your most important product or service? One change in the way that you appeal to your customers can transform your marketing and sales results overnight.

Competitive Analysis

IN MILITARY strategy, all decisions are made as the result of thinking about and understanding what your enemy is doing and is likely to do. Sometimes this is called "competitive response." It is a vital factor in your decision making in a competitive market.

For this reason, competitive analysis is one of the most important activities you can engage in. It is the starting point of differentiating your product or service from all of your competitors. It requires that you understand your competitor and the perceived benefits or qualities of his product or service at a deep level.

Identify Your Competitors

Who are your competitors? Your competition determines how much you will sell; where you will sell it; the size, quality, and your mix of products and services; and the profitability of your business. It will determine whether you succeed or fail, how much profit you will make on sales, and how much return you will earn on your investments.

Knowing your competition is critical. To use a military example again: You cannot win a military campaign without carefully considering and learning about your enemy, and then by using that knowledge to defeat your enemy in the open field or the open market.

You also need to ask yourself quite honestly why people buy from your competition. What benefit or advantage do they see in buying from your competition? What are the strengths possessed by your competition and what could you do to offset these strengths?

Why Should They Switch?

Another question with regard to your customers who are currently using your competition's products is: "Why should they switch?" Why should anybody switch from a supplier with whom they are satisfied to buy your product or service? You should be able to give the answer to this question in twenty-five words or less. If you cannot answer this question quickly and persuasively, it means that you probably don't know what the answer is.

It is generally agreed that you need at least three reasons for customers to switch from an existing supplier with whom they are quite satisfied to buy from you for the first time. What are those three reasons for your product or service? What could they be? How could you present them in such a way that they trigger buying action on the part of your ideal prospects?

One of your best sources of competitive analysis is to ask your noncustomers why it is that they prefer your competitors' products. Sometimes, they will give you insights that will enable you to modify your product or service to neutralize the perceived advantage possessed by your competition.

What Is Your Competition?

What is your competition? This is different from "Who is your competition?" Very often your competition is not another company that sells a similar product or service in competition against you; instead it can be market ignorance: People do not know about your product or service, and how much better off they can be when they use it. It could be that what you need is not to market and advertise against your competition, but to increase market awareness via public relations, advertising, and promotion.

When I worked for Carnival Cruise Lines as a speaker and trainer, I asked the company executives, "Who is your competition?" They were very clear about the answer. It was not other cruise lines at all. It was the habit of people to take land-based vacations instead of sea cruises. They felt that only 5 percent of the potential market for cruise passengers had been tapped, by all the cruise lines put together. Too many people were convinced that land-based vacations were superior. Their real competition was this perception of the difference between a vacation on land and a vacation at sea.

When I address my sales audiences, I point out to them that 80 percent of the customers that can buy from them are not even aware that their company or product exists in the marketplace. Even with all the advertising, promotion, and sales activity your company engages in, fully 80 percent of all the people who could buy your product or service are not even aware of your existence.

Challenge Your Assumptions

What are your critical assumptions about your competition? Errant assumptions lie at the root of most marketing failures. Could your assumptions about your competition be wrong? If they were wrong, what would you have to do differently?

We are living today in the age of the Apple iPhone and the Samsung Galaxy. In 2006, before these phones were introduced, Nokia had 49 percent of the cell phone market, and BlackBerry had another 29 percent, mostly in the business market.

When the first iPhone was announced in 2006 and released in 2007, both Nokia and BlackBerry made the same fatal error. They said, "The iPhone is just a toy; nobody wants to have a device that lets them communicate and connect with all their friends, plus have e-mail, messaging, and applications. It is a passing fad that we don't need to think about."

Today, both companies are finished. Because they had the wrong assumptions about the impact of the iPhone on the mobile phone market, they took two of the biggest and most profitable brands in the world and trashed them within five years.

What are your assumptions about your competition— including what they are doing now, and what they could be doing in the future?

The biggest mistake frequently made with regard to our competitors is not to respect them enough. We underestimate their intelligence, tenacity, and their desire to drive us into the sea in pursuit of market share and profitability. Always assume that your competition is smart, competent, caring, innovative, and thinking about the same things that you are thinking about in terms of winning customers. Don't ever underestimate them.

Ask yourself, "What are they doing right?" Once you know what they are doing right, which is enabling them to attract sales and market share, ask yourself how you could creatively imitate your competitors in order to be better than them in the eyes of your potential customer.

Who Is Your Noncompetitor?

One final point in competitive analysis is to examine your noncompetitors. Who is selling products and services to your customers but is not competing with you? Looking at your noncompetitors can sometimes open up your mind and allow you to see market opportunities that do not today exist.

Today, the use of strategic alliances and joint ventures with noncompetitors is a powerful marketing technique.

Find a successful supplier, a noncompetitor, who is selling products and services to exactly the kind of people who should be buying your products and services. Approach this supplier and make an offer. Tell them that if they will introduce you to their customers, you will introduce them to your customers.

Dell offered its computer products online and by telephone for most of its existence. Then one day it entered into a strategic alliance with Walmart. Sales increased by billions of dollars and made Dell temporarily the biggest personal computer manufacturer in the world. What kind of strategic alliance could you enter into with your products and services that would be a win-win arrangement for both parties?

The great military strategist Sun Tzu was famous for saying, "He who knows himself will win a few battles. He who knows the enemy will win even more battles. But he who knows both himself and the enemy will prevail in 100 battles."

When you know the strengths and weaknesses of your products and services, and you know the strengths, weaknesses, and likely actions or behaviors of your competitors, you will prevail in 100 market battles.

EIGHT

Achieving Competitive Advantage

AS WE SAID before, the purpose of marketing is to create perceptions of "unique added value" in the minds of your customers. To survive and grow, every product and service offering must have some clear, distinct competitive advantage over its competitors in the marketplace.

Competitive advantage is the key to sales success and high profitability. It is absolutely essential that you are excellent in some specific area that customers value. You have to be able to say to your customers, "We offer the very best for you in this critical area."

Everyone in your organization should know exactly where, why, and how your company and product or service is superior to every other competitor in the market. If you are not clearly superior than your competitors somewhere and somehow, in a market-specific area, then all that you can hope for is survival, if that.

The 80/20 Rule Revisited

Remember that old 80/20 rule? Twenty percent of the companies in every industry earn 80 percent of the profits. This means that 80 percent of the companies in an industry only earn 20 percent of the profits. Your goal, your main focus, is to get into the top 20 percent and then to move up as fast as you can in the months and years ahead.

All marketing and sales strategy is based on *differentiation*. It is based on showing your customers exactly how your products and services are different from and better than any other competitive products or services offered in the marketplace. What is your competitive advantage? What do you do or offer that makes your products or services superior to that of your competitors? What is your area of excellence? Jack Welch of General Electric was famous for saying that "if you don't have a competitive advantage, don't compete." Again, clarity is the most important word in this area. What is your competitive advantage today? What *will* your competitive advantage be in the future? What *should* your competitive advantage be if you want to stand out from your competitors? What *could* your competitive advantage be if you want to lead your industry in sales and profitability? And most important, what changes will you have to make immediately to develop and maintain a competitive advantage that enables you to achieve market supremacy?

The Black Belt Level

For many years, I trained in karate, up to the black belt level. I traveled and visited many karate schools and settled on Shotokan Karate. In my estimation, it was the very best karate school of the ten major karate schools offering lessons around the world.

Then I found something interesting. The students in every other karate school were absolutely convinced that their karate school was superior to all other karate schools. This attitude seems to apply to customers as well. I later discovered that every customer has exactly the same mind-set. Customers always buy what they perceive to be the very best choice for them in the marketplace, at any given time.

When customers buy a product or service, at the moment of purchase, they are convinced that this product or service is superior to any other competitive offering and is therefore the best choice for them. This conclusion may be based on reality or on perceptions created by advertising and promotion. It may be the result of price considerations, which is important to the customers of Walmart, and it may be based on other factors. But customers buy only when they are convinced that their purchase is the very best decision that they can make at that time, all things considered.

Uniqueness and Differentiation

This brings us back to the concepts of uniqueness and differentiation. How can you make your product offerings stand out from your competitors' products in a way that your customers will say: "This is a better product or service for me than anything else that is being offered?"

You define your competitive advantage—the reason for buying your products or services—in terms of the benefits, results, or outcomes that your customers will enjoy from purchasing your product or service, and that they would not fully enjoy from purchasing the product or service of your competitor.

Discovering, developing, and promoting your area of uniqueness is vital in attaining market leadership and superior profitability. This is sometimes called your "unique selling proposition." It is something that you offer that your customer values, and that no other competitor can offer, and that makes your product or service a more attractive choice than anything else available.

Your Unique Selling Proposition

This unique selling proposition should be made clear in all your promotional materials. It becomes the heart or core of all your advertising and marketing efforts. It is the single message that you strive to convey to your potential customers in every way possible.

Marketing success comes from you continually thinking about achieving and maintaining a sustainable competitive advantage. This is the critical focus for every successful business. All companies that achieve clear competitive advantage, and differentiation from their competition, eventually move up into the top 20 percent.

Unfortunately, if you do not have competitive advantage, if your product or service is a "me too" product or service, then the only way that you can sell it is by reducing the price. Soon you are among the other 80 percent of businesses that are also racing to the bottom by reducing the price. At the end of the day there is little or no profit for anyone. Most of these companies eventually go out of business because they cannot survive.

Don't let this happen to you. The best strategy for you and your company is to focus on improving the quality of your product or service so that it is universally recognized as being superior to anything else available. Once you have achieved this perception, you will sell more, at higher prices and at a lower cost of customer acquisition, and will enjoy greater repeat sales and referrals than with any other strategy.

NINE

The Marketing Mix

THE MARKETING mix is like a complex recipe for a special dish that you prepare in the kitchen. Each of the ingredients is essential. Each of the ingredients must be blended into the recipe in exactly the correct form and quantity, and at exactly the right time, for the dish to turn out tasting delicious.

There are seven Ps to the marketing mix. A change in any one of these ingredients can bring about a small or a large change in your business. Often, a change in one element of one part of the marketing mix can transform your business completely, from a small business to a large business, or if you are unlucky, from a large business into a small business. Let's take them in order.

The Product or Service

The first ingredient of the marketing mix is your product or service. This is the starting point. What exactly do you sell? The first part of the answer to this question is your product or service itself. What is it? How is it made? What does it do? What purpose does it serve, and so on?

The second part of the answer to this question "What is your product?" is what your product actually "does" to change, improve, or transform the life of your customer. This is the most important question that you must ask and answer for marketing success.

What would you say? Whatever your answer, this is the heart of your business.

The Price

The second part of the marketing mix is your pricing strategy. Exactly how much does your product or service cost to produce, including all direct and indirect expenses? On that basis, how much do you charge or must you charge in order to make enough of a profit to justify being in this business in the first place?

Your pricing strategy can make the difference between high and low profits. Sometimes, gradually increasing your prices by a few percentage points over the course of a year can dramatically affect your bottom line. Small but consistent reductions in your costs, without sacrificing quality, can boost your profitability substantially.

You may find that you have products or services where you are actually losing money each time you sell the product.

Sometimes, you can add a new product feature to your existing product and increase its perceived value and its price substantially. Sometimes you can remove a feature that your customers don't care about and reduce your costs, increasing your profits in that way.

Pricing strategy is something that you must visit and revisit continually, for each product or service, throughout the life of your business. Small changes in your pricing can lead to dramatic changes in your profitability.

The Promotion

The third part of the marketing mix is the promotion. This is an umbrella term that defines everything that you are going to do to inform your potential customers about your product or service and persuade them to buy it from you rather than from your competitors.

Promotion begins with your marketing strategy. Who is your customer? What does your customer consider value? What is the key benefit or advantage that your product or service offers that no other competitors can offer? How can you explain or illustrate exactly the most important reason that customers should buy from you? Your answer to this question, your *unique selling proposition*, becomes the heart and core of all your advertising and promotional activities.

The Place

The fourth P is the place at which you sell your product or service. How and where do customers acquire your product or service once they have decided to purchase it? Do they get it from you directly, from your office or store? Is it sent by mail or e-mail? Changing the place where you sell your product can dramatically change the volume of sales that you enjoy and the profitability that you generate.

Amazon has become the biggest online retailer in the world, largely because of the places it locates its warehouses and the resulting speed at which it delivers its products and services.

In what way could you change your location or place of business, or your way of delivering your product or service to your customer in such a way that it would be more convenient and attractive to your customers, and thereby increase your business and repeat business? This is one of the great questions that can make or break a business.

The Packaging

The fifth part of the marketing mix is packaging, which refers largely to the visual impression that is made by any and every part of your business on your potential customer.

People are intensely visual. Fully 95 percent of the first impression that a person gets of your business, your product, or your service will be based on what they see with their eyes. They then make a decision in approximately four seconds on whether your product or service is good, desirable, valuable, worth the price, and/or better than your competitors' product or service. In the next thirty seconds, they begin using what is called "confirmation bias." This is when they justify, rationalize, and firm up the decision that they made in the first four seconds of visual perception.

What could you do, starting today, to improve the packaging of any part of your business? How could you make the visual impression of your products, services, people, or business more attractive and appealing? How could you improve the look of your brochures, printed materials, and website so that people are immediately impressed with their attractiveness at the very first glimpse?

The Positioning

The sixth part of the marketing mix is your positioning. This is one of the key elements in marketing and sales today, and it is as important as any other factor. Your positioning refers to the way that your customers and noncustomers think about you and talk about you after they have used your products or services, and when you are not there.

Theodore Levitt, of the Harvard Business School, said that "a company's most valuable asset is its reputation."

Your reputation is defined as "the way you are known to others, especially to your customers."

How are your company and your products and services known to your customers? How are your products and services known or thought about by your noncustomers or your potential customers? It is essential that you know the answers to these questions and that you are working on improving these answers.

The People

The seventh part of the marketing mix is people. In the final analysis, people do not buy products from companies. They buy products from the people in those companies that sell them to them. In my sales seminars, I point out one of the golden rules of selling: "A customer will not buy from you until he is convinced that you are his friend and that you are acting in his best interests."

In our explanations of "relationship selling," we point out that it is how the customer feels about you—the personal and human contact—that largely determines whether the customer will buy from you or from a competitor. We only buy from people we like or who are like us in some way.

Your choice of the people who interact with your customers can be the single most important factor determining your success or failure. You must choose these people with tremendous care. Who are the key people inside and outside your business who determine your level of sales? Who are the people who make that lasting impression that determines how your customers think and feel about you when you are not there?

Successful marketing is based on the accurate determination of the correct marketing mix. If your product or service is not selling up to expectations, or if your company is not generating the profits that you desire, usually one or more factors in the marketing mix requires alteration. This mix needs to be continuously revised and rethought in order to yield the highest possible sales and the greatest possible productivity. And there are always multiple ways that you can improve one or more of these seven factors.

TEN

Positioning Strategies

POSITIONING IS a vital part of the marketing mix and of marketing strategy. A focus on positioning strategy means structuring your business in the marketplace so that you are perceived to be different and better than your competitors.

How do you want your product, service, and company to be viewed by your customers? What would you like them to say about you and your offerings? How would you like them to describe you to other people? If someone were to call one of your customers to ask for a referral or recommendation, how would you like to be talked about by your customer? And most important of all, how can you achieve this ideal perception in the hearts and minds of your customers?

What Words Do You Own?

Your positioning is contained in the words that customers use to describe you, and to describe your product and service to others. These are the words that are triggered when your company name, product, or service is mentioned or when the customer thinks of them during the course of a day.

What words do you own in your customers' minds? What words would it be helpful for you to own in your customers' minds? What words would cause your customers to buy from you more readily and to tell their friends to buy from you as well? Your answers to these questions cannot be left to chance. They are the critical determinant of your success or failure in business.

A Marketing Classic

Al Ries and Jack Trout wrote a book many years ago entitled *Positioning: The Battle for Your Mind.* It is now a classic of marketing literature that every person in business should read—even if it causes them to cringe a little as they go through it. What Ries and Trout identified was what is considered by most people to be the heartbeat of success in modern marketing.

Sit down with your key people and ask the question, "What words would we like people to use when they refer to us?" Then ask, "What would we have to do, starting today, to trigger those words in our customers' minds as the result of the impression they get when they do business with us?"

Leave Nothing to Chance

In his time, Sam Walton was the richest man in the world, worth more than $100 billion. He started off as a young man with a discount clothing store in Bentonville, Arkansas. He had one simple concept: He wanted his store to be perceived as one that cared about its customers and supplied good quality merchandise at fair prices. Not the lowest prices, but good quality at fair prices. He managed to achieve that perception to the point where he went on to make Walmart the most successful retailing operation in history.

What perception do you want to create? How would it be *useful* for you to be viewed by your customer? Would you like to be described as the quality leader? Service leader? Low price leader? Think in terms of how you want people to think and feel about you and your business. What could you do starting today to begin creating that perception?

IBM created the perception that it gave the finest customer service of any company in the world. That perception became so prevalent that people who didn't even know much about IBM would tell you that the company gave excellent customer service.

The perception that you generate on the outside can only be accomplished if you make fundamental critical changes on the inside of your business. In other words, you cannot create a false perception that will last for any period of time. A customer perception that endures must be a real reflection of the internal structure and values of your organization. It can only be based on the way that you treat your customers, every single time.

So once again, how can you position your product or service so that it stands out from your competitors? How can you get people to feel that your product or service is different, better, and worth paying for in competition with others?

ELEVEN

Four Principles of Marketing Strategy

ALL BUSINESS strategy is marketing strategy. Your ability to attract qualified prospects determines your success in business. You are responsible for making the critical strategic decisions for your business, especially in these four areas.

Specialization

This is the product, service, customer, market, or area of technology where you focus all your efforts. This becomes the "driving force" of your marketing, sales, and business activities.

You can specialize in a particular product and concentrate on offering something of unique added value in that product category that is better, faster, cheaper, and superior to that of your competitors.

In the same vein, you can have a service-driven focus on specialization. You can offer a specific service to a specific market group and concentrate on making your service the best, cheapest, most convenient, and most attractive of all people offering a similar service to the same customers.

You may have a customer-driven focus, such as that practiced by Walmart. Walmart focuses on customers who "live from paycheck to paycheck." Sam Walton's original idea was to offer good products at good prices to the vast majority of consumers in America, and in subsequent market areas that Walmart entered into.

You may aim at a specific market as your area of specialization. The market could be local, statewide, national, or even international. But when you choose a particular market area, your focus is to specialize in that area and to offer something of greater value than any of your competitors in the same area.

You may specialize in *technology*, or even in a specific capability that your company possesses that is not enjoyed by your competitors. Many companies specialize in a particular distribution channel, such as Amway, Avon, or Herbalife.

Differentiation

This is the heartbeat of marketing, and the primary reason for business success or failure. Your area of differentiation is where you set yourself apart from all other companies that compete to sell a similar product to the same customers.

Here is an exercise for you: Imagine that all your competitors suddenly disappeared from the market and you were left alone as the only supplier of your particular product or service. What difference would that make in your sales and profitability? I would guess that it would enable you to become one of the most successful and profitable businesses in your industry, if not in the world.

Here is the question: How can you differentiate your product or service in such a way that, as far as the customer is concerned, you are the "only choice" in buying this product or service in today's market?

Segmentation

Many marketing experts today say that all of marketing in the future will depend on your ability to segment your market accurately. The billions of dollars spent on market research each year are largely aimed at determining with some precision exactly who the customer is who will buy your product or service in competition against other companies who want that same customer.

The question is: "Who are those customers, exactly, who most appreciate your area of specialization and your area of uniqueness or superiority, and who want exactly those features and benefits that you are most capable of delivering?"

How would you describe your perfect or ideal customer? Who exactly is your target market; those customers in the ocean of customers who can and will most readily buy from you because of the unique added value that you offer or that you can offer by modifying your product or service in some way?

Begin with their demographics. What is the age of your ideal customer? Gender? Income range? Education? Occupation or profession? Where do your ideal customers live or work? And what is their family status or level of family formation?

The second part of defining your ideal customer is perhaps more important. It is what we call the "psychographics." It is what is going on inside the mind of your ideal customer that is going to have the greatest impact on whether the customer buys from you, buys from someone else, or does not buy at all.

What exactly are the main goals and ambitions of your ideal prospect? What are his wants, needs, and motivations for making a buying decision? What are her hopes, dreams, and aspirations for the future that your product or service can help her to realize?

What are this customer's fears, doubts, or worries that your product or service can take away, or that may stand in the way of the person buying from you?

Especially, what are the problems in the life of your ideal customer that your product or service can solve? What needs can your product or service satisfy? What goals can it help them to achieve? What pain can it take away from your ideal customer?

Concentration

This is the fourth pillar of marketing strategy, which flows naturally from your developing absolute clarity about your areas of specialization, differentiation, and segmentation. You know what you offer and what you don't offer. You know the reason or reasons why people should buy from you rather than from someone else. You have identified the ideal customer for your product or service offering. Now, the fourth stage is for you to concentrate single-mindedly on only those customers who can and will buy from you within a reasonable period of time.

What are the best possible ways for you to advertise and communicate with your ideal customers?

What are the best possible media that will allow you to communicate with the greatest number of potential customers at the lowest possible price? Most of all, what are the most powerful appeals that you can make that will trigger immediate or even instant buying responses?

Your Marketing Plan

When you combine the seven parts of the marketing mix with the four elements of marketing strategy, you will emerge with a great marketing plan.

A great marketing plan has several advantages. First of all it attracts a steady stream of qualified prospects, a river of potential customers flowing to your website or place of business. A great marketing plan emphasizes your unique selling proposition over and over, constantly communicating to customers exactly what it is that you offer in the form of "unique added value" that makes you the best and only choice to purchase your product or service.

Marketing is extremely complex in a highly competitive market, but at the same time, it is quite simple. Determine exactly who your ideal customers are and what they want. And then find a way to give them what they want, better, faster, and cheaper than your competitors.

TWELVE

Choosing the Battlefield

YOUR SELLING and marketing strategy means choosing who you will compete against and on what basis.

If you decide to change your product offerings or your markets, and the customers to whom you are offering your products and services, you change who your competition will be. Just as if you are a country surrounded by other countries and you decide to go to war, it is the direction of your attack that is going to determine all your planning.

Change Your Customer, Change Your Competition

A perfect example again is the Steve Jobs/iPhone decision to compete in a completely new area of technology and innovation than Apple had ever been involved in before. Apple saw an opportunity to produce a mobile phone that was completely different from what was being offered in the market, and to introduce new technologies that improved the quality and enjoyability of the phone far beyond anything that Nokia, BlackBerry, or Sony Ericsson were producing.

In choosing the battlefield, you begin with your customer. What is it that your customers of today are asking for or will be wanting in the years ahead? How could you develop or adapt new technologies to satisfy the customer of tomorrow? All market planning begins with thinking about the customer and what you need to do to make that customer happy.

You may decide to change your customer, and go after a market that is either underserved or not being properly served by your competitors. By choosing new customers to satisfy, or new products or services to offer to your existing and future customers, you completely change the nature of your marketing battlefield. You change the future of your business.

Strengths vs. Weaknesses

Ask yourself, "What are the strengths and weaknesses of my competition in my existing market and in the new markets that I could enter?"

The strength of BlackBerry was its enormous success in providing telephones for businesspeople. Its great weakness was that it became so convinced of its superiority that it stopped technological innovation and became a sitting duck for the Apple iPhone and the Samsung Galaxy when they came along. From being a market leader to bankruptcy was five short years. It would not have happened if the makers of the BlackBerry had devoted as much time, money, and research to improving their product as they did to rewarding themselves with bonuses and dividends.

What are the strengths and weaknesses of your competitors? How could you minimize their strengths and exploit their weaknesses? Where do their strengths and weaknesses offer you market opportunities that nobody perceives at this time?

Simultaneously, you identify your own strengths, and look for ways to compensate for your weaknesses relative to your competition.

Think about competitive response, the actions that your enemy will take to defend and protect his sales and revenue, his customers. If you decide to enter the marketplace with a new product or service, or enter a new marketplace with your existing product or service, or increase your advertising budget to go after greater market share, what are your competitors likely to do? They will not sit there passively allowing you to invade their market, as BlackBerry did.

Preserve Your Resources

One of the most famous battles in ancient history was between the Roman army and the Greek army, under King Pyrrhus. At the end of the battle, the forces of Pyrrhus had defeated the Romans but at a cost of about 50 percent of his army.

When someone congratulated him for winning this great battle against the Romans, he made the famous remark that has been quoted throughout history: "One such victory more and I am undone."

The next year, the Romans came back. Another battle took place. But the forces of Pyrrhus had been so devastated by winning the first battle that he was completely overwhelmed by the fresh Roman army, and lost both his kingdom and his life.

In business, it is very important that we do not achieve a "pyrrhic victory." It is very important that if you are going to achieve a certain level of market superiority, it does not cost you so much money that the victory is really hollow at the end of the day.

Change Your Product and Competition Carefully

Changing your business changes your competitor, and changing your competitor changes your business. Remember that the actions and reactions of your competitors will determine your growth, market share, and profitability. As a good strategist, you must study your competitors carefully and determine exactly what they might do in response to anything that you do to enter new markets or to introduce new products and services. You should also determine if you can win substantial market share against the new competitor you are thinking of challenging.

THIRTEEN

Military Principles of Marketing Strategy

THE MOST important skill that you have as a marketer is your ability to think better than your competitors. Each idea that you have in your mental toolbox gives you an advantage in enabling you to think differently and better than others. There are seven key principles of marketing strategy that you can use to improve your marketing efforts.

The Principle of the Objective

This is the starting point of marketing strategy, and perhaps the most important part of strategy in life. We said earlier that the most important word in business success is *clarity*. This requires that you be absolutely clear about your goals and objectives for each of your marketing efforts.

Think on paper. Establish clear objectives in terms of your plan and organization, the costs and resources necessary to conduct your marketing activities, and the exact financial results that you anticipate or hope for. Hold your own feet to the fire. Measure yourself and set benchmarks against which you can compare your performance. Remember, "You can't hit a target that you can't see. What gets measured gets done."

Clearly define your marketing objectives and attach numbers and dates to them. Then, continually strive to "hit your numbers" and to improve upon your performance.

The Principle of the Offensive

Napoleon said, "No great battles are ever won on the defensive." For you to be successful in marketing you must practice the "continuous offensive." You must be constantly trying new things and discarding old ideas that do not work.

There seems to be a direct relationship between the number of new ideas that you attempt in marketing and the likelihood that you will find the ideal way to present your product or service that will cause the telephone or the cash register to ring.

Beware the lure of the "comfort zone." Many people use a marketing method that brings them a modicum of success, and they soon fall in love with it and resist change for any reason. This is not for you. You must be continually looking for ways to improve your marketing results. And there are always ways to achieve this goal. Your need is to find them.

The Principle of the Mass

Great battles are won by concentrating your forces at the enemy's area of weakness. Your ability to focus and concentrate on your very best message, and aim it at your very best customer, is an essential key to marketing success.

The Principle of the Maneuver

To maneuver in military terms means to move quickly and to be ready to try different approaches and methods of attack. In marketing, we refer to maneuver as creativity and innovation—finding better, faster, and more attractive ways to communicate with our customers and get them to consider buying our product or service.

Practice zero-based thinking. Ask the question: "Is there anything that I am doing in my marketing efforts that, knowing what I now know, I wouldn't start up again today?"

Be prepared to hold yourself to a high standard. Be prepared to abandon methods and techniques of marketing that may have worked in the past but are no longer working today.

An excellent way to expand your creativity in marketing is to study the advertising and promotional efforts of your most successful competitors and noncompetitors. When I started writing advertising for a large agency, I spent many, many hours studying the most successful advertisements in history, and the most successful advertising executives and copywriters. It is amazing how much you can learn by continually exposing yourself to the most successful efforts of others.

The Principle of Concerted Effort

In military terms, concerted effort means the coordination of all forces simultaneously when conducting an attack on the enemy. In business, this refers to teamwork. In marketing, the idea of concerted effort refers to your working closely with everyone who is involved in the marketing effort, from the people developing the product or service in the first place, all the way through to the salespeople and the customer service representatives who talk to your end customers after they have bought and used the product.

Alfred P. Sloan, the superb executive who assembled and built General Motors into one of the biggest companies in the world, would disappear from his office for as much as a week every month. No one knew where he had gone, and when he came back, he said nothing.

Later, it was discovered that Sloan would drive several hundred miles from Detroit and work for a week in a General Motors car dealership, talking to and interacting with customers, getting their candid comments and observations on the strengths and weaknesses of the current General Motors offerings. Sloan would then go back to his office fully informed, and much better informed than his executives, and was able to guide GM to make excellent decisions in design and marketing.

A very important part of your team effort is to involve your customers. Invite continuous feedback from them about your product or service; ask how they think and feel about it. I teach this concept over and over again: "Your customers will make you rich, if you ask them enough questions and listen to their answers."

Your goal should be to involve everyone in your organization that touches your customers in any way, and continually elicit feedback that will enable you to communicate with those customers more effectively. One idea coming from one person can transform the results of your marketing efforts.

The Principle of Surprise

In military terms, all great victories are won as the result of doing something that the enemy never expected. In World War II, the Allied forces landed at Normandy when they were expected at Calais. The Germans attacked through the almost impassable Ardennes forest when they were expected to attack much farther north.

Apple announced its new iPhone to the world market and caught both Nokia and BlackBerry completely off guard, leading to their subsequent "defeat" or demise in the cell phone market.

What marketing strategies could you implement that would catch your competitors by complete surprise? What message or offering could you present that would cause potential customers of your product or service to move in large numbers toward buying from you?

The Principle of Exploitation

In military terms, this refers to the strategy of following through with your entire force when you achieve a breakthrough of any kind. In marketing, it refers to your fully exploiting any breakthrough that you can achieve in your market as the result of an excellent marketing message or approach.

When you develop a marketing message that gets extraordinary results, double up and triple up as fast as you can on your marketing to take full advantage of your new position in the marketplace. Remember, your competitors are going to respond quickly and aggressively, so you cannot waste any time when you achieve a success or a breakthrough.

Think of yourself as a general in command of your "marketing forces." Think continually about how you can deploy and redeploy your resources to achieve victories in the game of "marketing warfare."

FOURTEEN

Marketing Tactics of Diversion and Dissuasion

HOW CAN you utilize your strengths to gain a superior position in the marketplace? If you are starting out with a good product or service, and you see an opportunity to sell a lot of it at a good price and profit, you must then be sure that your competitors don't see what you are doing and rush in to compete for the same customer.

It is a law of economics that whenever there are "above market profits," competitors will rush into that marketplace to offer their goods and services. For example, in real estate markets, whenever a boom starts, individual entrepreneurs, without coordination with each other, rush in to build and offer more homes and properties. Soon, the market is oversaturated and the high prices that attracted competitors turn into low prices that often force competitors out of business.

Don't Tempt Your Competitors

Your competitors will enter into any marketplace where they perceive that there are above-average profits to be made. Everything that you can do to deflect their attention away from your potential or real profitability gives you a longer and stronger position in the marketplace.

If ever a competitor or someone you're not sure about asks you how your business is going, always tell them that it's a constant struggle. "The market is really tough today. We are fighting for every dollar."

Appear Unworthy of Attention

The first strategy when you enter into a potentially profitable market is to appear unworthy of attention. Appear to be too small and insignificant, and give the impression that you are going after a very small market segment.

Whether this was Apple's strategy with the iPhone, I don't know. But it might very well have been because its competitors dismissed the iPhone and ignored Apple's marketing activities until it was too late. The second action is that, when you do achieve high levels of sales profits, don't make big announcements or brag about your success until you are so far ahead of your competition that they can never catch you. Don't wave a red flag in the face of a bull of aggressive competitors.

Many companies use the strategy of establishing themselves strongly in the market and then announcing that they are now so large, strong, and fully entrenched that their competition should go somewhere else. Sometimes this strategy is successful, and sometimes it is not, but the perception of suddenly achieving market dominance in a particular product or service offering will often cause your competitors to look elsewhere for sales and profitability.

Keep Your Plans Secret

Be secretive, especially with new product offerings or where you see tremendous market opportunities. Be as secretive as possible until you are ready to launch, just as Apple practiced almost obsessive secrecy before the launch of the iPod, iPhone, and iPad. When these products were launched, they sold many millions of units within a few months.

Apple has built a reputation for tightly controlling and protecting its internal information before the introduction of new products.

Using military strategy again, you don't want your rivals to see you "assembling your armies." This was a strategy practiced by Napoleon. By massing his forces in secret, he was able to win major battle after major battle in one of the longest and most successful military careers in history.

Napoleon would deliberately keep his army divisions separate and apart over a wide geographic area until he was ready for a major battle. He would then have all his divisions converge and mass simultaneously in a single place for battle. He would often consolidate his armies in as little as twenty-four or forty-eight hours, to the complete surprise of the enemy. When he offered battle he almost always had numerical superiority at the point of contact. He was able to overwhelm virtually every army of Europe because he was able to remain obscure until he was ready to reveal himself and launch his full army.

This should be the same with you. Keep your product and service development activities quiet. Act as if you are going about your regular business. Impose a blanket of secrecy on your new products so that your competitors have no idea what you are likely to do. In military terms, surprise is an essential strategy for great victory in the marketplace.

Redirect Their Attention

Look for ways to redirect the attention of your competitors away from your major products, services, and markets. If you have a high-profit product and low-profit products, when people ask you how business is going, redirect their attention to your low-profit, high-volume products so that your competitors begin to think that is where the market is, and that's where they should be channeling their energies. Encourage your competitors to go after the markets that are least profitable for you. Remaining secret and private about your most profitable product areas is a key marketing strategy.

The natural tendency of many businesses is to blow their own horns, to brag about their market successes. They make loud public announcements about the areas where they are earning the highest profits. They wave the red flag in front of the bull and encourage their competitors to rush into those markets with their own products or services, even if the competitive quality is not as good. Eventually, their sales, profits, and market share decline. This is what happens when you encourage other competitors into your marketplace.

FIFTEEN

Practice the "Firstest with the Mostest" Strategy

NATHAN BEDFORD Forrest enrolled as a private and subsequently became a cavalry general for the Confederate Army during the Civil War. His unconventional approaches to warfare enabled him to achieve a string of victories that were unprecedented among the Southern forces. One of his favorite approaches was "firstest with the mostest."

He believed that the general who could mass all of his troops simultaneously at a single place before the enemy became aware of what he was doing would achieve the necessary superiority to win. And he was right, time after time. He was constantly moving his forces around to deceive the enemy and then bringing them together and massing them at a critical point where he would overwhelm the Northern forces every time.

In marketing, this refers to the strategy of developing a superior product or service and then getting it out into the marketplace everywhere, all at once, before your competition is even aware of what is happening.

This strategy is aimed at market leadership, to enable you to become number one in your market segment. It is not only a high-risk strategy, but it is also potentially the highest-profit strategy.

The "firstest with the mostest" strategy is ideal for a new product or service with a distinct competitive advantage or uniqueness that differentiates it from anything else being offered in the current market. This strategy allows you to gain an immediate market advantage by using two of the most powerful principles of strategy: surprise and exploitation.

The Surprise Principle

As described in Chapter 13, the surprise principle in warfare is taking an action that is not anticipated by the enemy. There are many ways to apply the surprise principle in business, such as combining your products to create new, more valuable offerings or breaking down your products to make them more affordable to more customers. Sometimes, companies gain an advantage by abandoning one market altogether and concentrating their resources in a different market—the equivalent of General Forrest moving his troops to where they were not expected.

Unfortunately, many leaders undermine the surprise principle in their own companies because they create an environment that punishes risk taking. If your managers or your employees are afraid of doing anything new because they are never allowed to fail, your company will have little chance of ever surprising the competition.

The Exploitation Principle

The exploitation principle relates to taking full advantage of a victory. Military leaders will immediately take full advantage of any kind of a breakthrough or advantage, pouring their resources into the opening that's been achieved to gain a decisive victory. The same approach should be applied in business: Any breakthrough should be immediately followed up with a concerted action, whether that means upselling to new customers or initiating a new product development program on the heels of a successful product launch.

The Apple Strategy

Apple exemplifies the success of the "firstest with the moistest" strategy. Each time Apple announces a new product or an improvement on an existing product, it builds up the market suspense so that the entire world is watching and waiting. Then, almost overnight, the new product is available worldwide. Using this strategy with the iPhone 5S and 5C, Apple sold more than 9 million sets within seventy-two hours of the product release, generating billions of dollars in sales and profits, much to the dismay of Apple's major competitors.

In what way could you use the "firstest with the mostest" strategy to introduce a new product or service throughout your entire market area, virtually overnight? The competition is watching. How can you outsmart them?

SIXTEEN

Use the "Hit 'Em Where They Ain't" Strategy

THIS IS often called a "white space strategy." You look at your market and you identify a product or service that no one is offering that would fit neatly in the white space between what currently exists and what you can bring to the market.

When Domino's Pizza began, there were thousands of pizzerias offering the standard menu of pizza dishes, including in the same market area where the first Domino's Pizza was established.

The white space that the founder of Domino's, Tom Monaghan, identified was that when customers ordered pizza, speed was more important than quality. When a customer phoned in a pizza order, he was *already* hungry and wanting to eat as soon as possible. Monaghan filled this white space by offering pizza delivery within thirty minutes, and then restructured the entire process of producing pizzas to enable his company to hit that goal.

The rest is history. Today there are more than 8,000 Domino's Pizza restaurants around the world, and Tom Monaghan has long since comfortably retired with a fortune of almost $2 billion. This is not a bad result for identifying a white space that was clear and obvious to everyone, but which all competitors ignored except for Domino's.

Offer Something Better, Faster, Cheaper

Look for ways to introduce a new product or service combination into an existing marketplace where nobody is offering that particular product or service. Do something different and unexpected in the marketplace. You can create an imitation product and do your competitors one better. By practicing creative imitation, you take what your competitors are doing and improve on it in order to leap ahead in market perception.

Another example of hitting 'em where they ain't was when a toothpaste company in a crowded market added an antiplaque formula and almost overnight relegated standard toothpastes to a second-rate status.

Very soon afterward, Colgate introduced a whitening formula in its toothpaste that no one else was offering, and also quickly relegated many of its competitors to second-rate status.

Just imagine! You go to the store to buy toothpaste for yourself and your family and you have a choice between standard toothpaste, antiplaque toothpaste, or a toothpaste with a whitening formula. Which one would you choose? And very quickly thereafter, another company came out with a toothpaste that had both an antiplaque formula and a whitening formula, and the race was on once more.

Reposition Your Product

You can also hit 'em where they ain't by perfecting and repositioning your product. For many years, the soft drink 7Up struggled in competition against Coke and Pepsi. The soft drink maker then shifted strategy completely and positioned 7Up as the "uncola."

Instead of competing against Coke and Pepsi, the maker emphasized that 7Up was a light, citrus, tangy drink as opposed to a dark-colored cola.

By repositioning in this way, they were able to increase their market share from 14 percent of the soft drink market to 20 percent in just a few years, representing hundreds of millions of dollars of increased sales and profitability.

Offer More Than Your Competitors

Another famous slogan based on repositioning was the Avis car rental ad that said, in comparison with Hertz, the world giant, "We're second; we try harder."

This message connected with potential customers who not only wanted to give the underdog a chance, but who recognized that if Avis "tried harder" the customer would probably get a better deal. Avis's sales grew and grew, eventually making the company number two in the rental car marketplace, even though it had never been number two in its history.

Another way you can hit 'em where they ain't is by adding something new and different to your product to make it entirely different from the existing product, thereby differentiating it from your competitors. You could add an accessory or an additional service that increases the value and attractiveness of what you offer and changes customer perceptions of your company.

Offer Something New

When Apple introduced the iPhone, it also did something completely revolutionary. In contrast to the long-held profit strategy of Apple, which was to keep all technology proprietary and in-house, it threw open its architecture to allow people to develop applications for the iPhone. Within a few months, the dam broke. Today there are more than 800,000 applications available for an iPhone, more than for any other smartphone on the market, and many of the application developers have become multimillionaires and even billionaires.

Today, there are more than one million entrepreneurs working alone or together to develop the next new "killer app" for the iPhone as well as Android phones, all hoping to fill a "white space" with a new service that will generate tremendous market usage and potentially a new entrepreneurial fortune.

SEVENTEEN

Dominate a Market Niche

YOU USE this strategy when you dominate a deep market niche with a product or service that everyone wants and has to have. You become the high-quality unique supplier of a product or service that everyone wants and no one is offering.

For example, smartphone users quickly went from e-mail to SMS messaging. But SMS messaging takes time and concentration, which is why it is largely banned from the nation's highways. To fill the market niche for the desire of cell phone users to communicate instantly and easily with their friends and associates, two companies quickly developed new applications, WeChat and WhatsApp.

With either of these apps, you can tap on the icon, quickly tap on the name of the desired recipient of your message, and dictate a message that will be transmitted in seconds, anywhere in the world. In no time at all, WeChat had over 200 million users (primarily in China), and WhatsApp has become the dominant app for voice communications in the rest of the world.

Create Something Essential

Another example of this strategy is called the "toll gate niche." This is where you develop a product or service that anyone in a particular business or industry needs to have in order to get the most value out of another product or service that is essential to their business or personal life.

My favorite example of this "toll gate" niche strategy is Hughes Drilling, established by the father of Howard Hughes many years ago. He was the first inventor to design, develop, and market a diamond drill bit for oil well drilling.

At one time, someone asked him if they really needed a Hughes diamond drill bit (which was very expensive). His response was that oil drillers always had two choices. They could use his bit to drill for oil, or they could use a shovel.

Within a couple of years, every oil drilling company in the world had no choice but to ante up and pay the prices that Hughes demanded. His drills were absolutely essential for cost-effective oil drilling.

Develop a Specialty Service

Another strategy is for you to develop a specialty skill or service that is so important that nobody else can do without it and still get the same result. A perfect example is Microsoft, which developed a suite of office programs that people needed to get results in their businesses efficiently and effectively. Microsoft then constantly improved its suite of programs, adding new features and simultaneously lowering the price so that no other competitor could get into the market.

This strategy of creating a product that became indispensable to efficient business operations, increasing its quality, and continually lowering its price, enabled Bill Gates to become the richest man in America, with a fortune today (2014) estimated at $72 billion.

How could you reposition one or more of your existing products in such a way that it becomes absolutely indispensible to anyone using another product or service? How could you dominate a market niche with something that is better, faster, and cheaper than anything else available?

Continually remind yourself of the concept of the need for "unique added value." Your central focus is to both develop and then to demonstrate that what you offer includes a unique added value that customers simply must have if they are going to be happy and satisfied.

EIGHTEEN

Creative Marketing Growth Strategies

HOW CAN you grow your markets? There are five basic creative marketing growth strategies.

First, you can sell more of your existing products in your existing markets by modifying them, advertising them more effectively, bundling them, unbundling them, expanding your distribution channels, or lowering your price. Which of these different strategies could you use to sell more of your existing products in your current markets?

Second, you can sell new products and services into your existing markets to your existing customers. Think of what other offerings you could create that complement your current products and services where you already have established credibility and distribution channels.

What additional wants, needs, and desires do your current customers have that you could satisfy with new products and services that would be complementary to what you already sell?

Remember, fully 80 percent of products being bought and used in five years will be different from today. The rate of product obsolescence today is faster than it's been in human history, except for the months and years ahead. You must continually be developing new products and services to replace those that have passed their due date in the current market.

Enter New Markets

Third, offer your existing products into new markets that you have never exploited before. Look for different markets that you could target with your products, both nationally and internationally.

Remember, 80 percent of your potential customers are not even aware that your product or service exists and how much better off they could be if they bought from you.

Fourth, and often the most difficult strategy, is for you to develop new products for new markets. The Apple story, with the iPod, iPhone, and iPad making Apple at one time the most valuable company in the world, is a perfect example of new products for new markets.

Another example might be Facebook, which went from an idea to more than a billion customers in less than ten years and made a large number of people extremely wealthy.

Mark Zuckerberg and his partners sensed that there was a great need for people to quickly and efficiently use technology to communicate and connect with other people over a wide area. From this basic idea, Facebook has expanded the wide range and variety of connection activities that are possible for a subscriber, making it one of the most successful and fastest-growing business ventures in history.

What new products and services could you develop for new markets using your existing capabilities, resources, manpower, and production capabilities? Think outside the box.

A final strategy is for you to identify excellent products and services produced by other companies that would be ideal for your existing customers. You can enter into joint ventures and strategic alliances to become a marketing channel for the products and services produced by other people. This can be a low-risk, high-profit strategy that you can implement on a trial basis initially.

Utilize Other Ways to Sell

THERE ARE probably thirty different ways to sell a product or service. Unfortunately, the average company falls in love with one or perhaps two different ways of selling its products, and then focuses only on those methods and strategies. In so doing, companies miss enormous potential sales opportunities.

Today, there are several different ways that you can sell your product or service on the Internet. In addition, there are telephone sales, small and large retail sales, direct selling, wholesale, catalogs, newspapers, franchises, through distributors, multilevel, in-home sales, television, radio, and other media sales, including mobile, as well as through joint ventures, strategic alliances, or even at trade shows.

Thousands of companies sell millions and billions of dollars' worth of products or services with one or more of these different methods of sale every year. If you are only using one or two of these methods, just one additional way of selling your offerings could double your business and make you a market leader.

Find Opportunities Through Distribution Channels

Distribution channels are how you get the merchandise from your business to the final end user. The ways of getting products to the marketplace are more important than the products themselves, in many cases. Distribution channels exist and endure long after products and services have become obsolete and left the market.

What additional products could you sell through your existing distribution channels? Let us say, for example, that your distribution channel is through your website. What additional methods of sale could you offer online that may be different or complementary to what you are offering today? What additional distribution channels would suit your current offerings?

Look at what your competitors are doing. Are they using different distribution channels than you? Sometimes changing your distribution channel can make a significant difference in the quantity of the products and services that you are selling into the marketplace.

What new products or services could you create for your existing distribution channels? Could you create and develop new products and services consistent with your existing product lines?

What products that are completely different from anything you've ever offered could you create for new or existing distribution channels?

A Success Story

For example, for many years, Avon had one of the most successful cosmetic retailing businesses in the world by having its distributors out knocking on doors and making direct sales in the homes of their customers. Ladies went from door to door doing product demonstrations, left catalogs, took orders, and sold hundreds of millions of dollars of product in this way.

However, the market changed. More and more of these female customers went into the workplace. So Avon started to call on offices rather than on homes, and the ladies who were now going from home to home began to go from office to office with the same products. They changed from residential sales to office and commercial sales.

At the same time, Avon upgraded and changed the cosmetics, making them more attractive and desirable, and then added jewelry and other accessories that working women wanted and were willing to buy. As a result, Avon became the most successful direct marketing company in the world.

Both IBM and Dell revolutionized their computer businesses and increased their sales by billions of dollars by offering their proprietary products through retail outlets owned by other companies. Both companies had always kept the sales and delivery process internal. When they began offering their products via retail, they exposed them to millions of additional potential customers. They were able to double and triple their market penetration in personal computers and in other devices.

For many years, Apple sold all of its products online, directly and through retail outlets. Then it began to open up Apple retail stores, using the very finest market research, lighting, layout, and technology to create what is today the most exemplary buying and selling experience in retail in the world.

Up until the Apple retail stores opened, with their incredible sensitivity and focus on customer satisfaction and indirect selling, the jeweler Tiffany's of New York was the highest-grossing retail company at $2,600 per square foot. Today, however, Apple stores gross $4,600 per square foot, and they do it all by "selling without selling."

Professionalize the Sales Process

How do you actually sell your product or service? What is the specific selling process from the first customer contact by e-mail, phone, or face-to-face, and what exactly do people ask and say at each stage of the process?

In most small companies, everyone says whatever comes to their mind at every customer contact. There is no consistency or uniformity. Sales results are also inconsistent and unpredictable. But as companies grow, they realize that they need a proven sales process that everyone follows, from the first customer contact through to the conclusion of the sale and the delivery of the product.

Most successful companies place heavy emphasis on the professionalism of their sales activities. In fact, a company with a thoroughly trained professional sales force can actually sell higher quantities and charge higher prices than a company with what might be a better product, but that is sold in a random and haphazard way.

Small changes in the way you market (which is the way you attract interested prospects) and sell (which is how you convert interested prospects into actual buyers) can dramatically improve your sales and profitability. Better sales and marketing can make all the difference between a small and a large company.

In every large national company, there are branches where they sell five and ten times as much as the average sold in other branches, even though the number of salespeople, the size of the market, and the prices of the products are the same. In every case, this is because the salespeople are thoroughly trained and carefully managed so that their sales activities are consistent and predictable.

TWENTY

The Bundle of Resources Concept

ONE OF the most important of all marketing concepts is called "the bundle of resources concept." As a mental exercise, look upon your company as a bundle of resources that is capable of producing and selling many products and services, not just the ones you are offering today.

Focus primarily on human, intellectual, and production resources. With these in mind, what new products or services could you produce with your existing people, skills, equipment, and financial structure to appeal to new customers in new markets?

Looking upon your business as a bundle of resources can help free you from the limitation of thinking only in terms of the products and services you are now offering, to the customers and markets that you are now serving. Think of your bundle of resources as being capable of producing a variety of profitable products and services for other profitable markets.

New Products Altogether

One of the best examples of this bundle of resources concept is Intel. In the 1970s and 1980s, Intel became the world leader in computer chips used in virtually every large and small consumer device, including toasters and washing machines, to improve efficiency. But then the Koreans and Taiwanese entered the market with computer chips of the same or better quality at vastly lower prices, bringing Intel to a moment of truth.

The people at Intel, including then president Andrew Grove, realized that there was no future for them in computer chips. They then made a decision to shift the entire business into the manufacture of microchips for computers. This required Intel to sell off its earlier chip manufacturing facilities, hundreds of millions of dollars' worth of factories, and shift all its resources into the construction of new factories producing new products for the growing personal computer market.

As you can imagine, they met with tremendous resistance, both internally, from the engineers and staff whose livelihoods would be affected by the shift, and externally, from customers and competitors in the marketplace. But Grove stuck to his guns and pushed through the transition. In a few years, the words "Intel Inside" became the "gold standard" for personal computers, and Intel went on to become one of the most successful and profitable companies in the world.

Explore Your Options

Perhaps you need to start a new business or division to explore new possibilities to develop and sell new products and services to new markets with new distribution channels. An open, flexible mind is essential in marketing. Many companies that are successful today may be selling something totally different five or ten years from now—and probably will be. In addition, new products and services may offer greater profit opportunities than anything that you have ever done up until now.

What are the trends? Where is the market going? What do your customers need today that you are not currently offering them and that you have the capability to offer them? What will your customers want in the future, and how can you begin developing new products and services so that you are ready for your customers when they get there?

TWENTY-ONE

Four Ways to Change Your Business

IN BUSINESS, and in life, there are only four ways that you can bring about substantial changes.

The first way is that you can "do more of some things." What should you be doing more of? The answer is that you should be doing more of those things from which you are getting the best results; those things that are succeeding; those activities that bring you the very highest and most predictable levels of sales and profitability.

It is amazing how many companies ignore this basic principle. They spend equal amounts of time and money promoting their entire product line rather than identifying those products and services that have the potential to be extremely successful and profitable in the marketplace if they receive enough time and attention.

The second way that you can change is by "doing less" of other things. And what should you be doing less of? The answer is simple. You should be doing less of those things that are bringing you fewer results than the other things that you are doing.

Keep applying the 80/20 rule to your business. Fully 80 percent of your products and services are contributing only 20 percent of your sales and profitability. Many companies have a strategic policy to discontinue 10 percent or 20 percent of their product line each year, and simultaneously have a goal to have 20 percent of their sales coming from new products and services each year.

The first two ways to change your business and improve your sales are to do more of some things and less of others. What should you be doing more of or less of?

Break Out of Your Comfort Zone

The third way to change your sales and marketing results is to start doing something completely new and different. This is one of the most difficult actions of all. Most people are stuck in a "comfort zone" that they struggle and strive to remain in, no matter what is going on around them.

This explains the "not invented here" syndrome that causes companies like Nokia, which developed much of the original technology for the iPhone and the iPad, to reject those technologies because they were afraid it might cut into their existing business.

This is a major weakness in marketing and sales. Companies fall in love with their existing products or services and then resist and push away other products and services that may eat into their existing business. This is what caused the downfall of BlackBerry and Nokia, and it causes the decline and downfall of companies of all sizes, all over the world every year.

So what do you need to start doing in order to survive and thrive in today's market? In their excellent book *Competing for the Future*, Gary Hamel and C. K. Prahalad wrote that every company should be projecting forward five years into the future and planning for market dominance at that time. You should do the same regularly, as an exercise in thinking.

Create Your Own Future

You then come back to the present day in your thinking and ask, "What will we have to start doing today to lead our industry five years from now?"

What additional products and services will we need? What additional skills and competences will we need? What will we need to do more of or less of? What will we need to start doing, and start immediately, to be ready to be market leaders five years from now?

Starting something new is one of the hardest things of all. It's why Confucius wrote, "A journey of a thousand leagues begins with a single step." For you to start anything new in your business, the first step is always the most difficult. But the first step is always the most necessary if you are going to create the future rather than be a victim of the future.

Michael Kami, the strategic planner, said these famous words: "Those who do not plan for the future cannot have one."

There is another saying: "To achieve something you have never achieved before, you will have to do something you've never done before. You'll have to develop skills you never had before. You will have to offer products and services that you never offered before. You will have to become a different person than you have ever been before."

Practice Zero-Based Thinking

The fourth way to change your life and work is to stop doing certain things altogether. There are many activities that consume your time and money that may have been valuable at one time, but are no longer valuable and important. Because of the influence of the comfort zone, many people waste a lot of their time doing things that need not be done at all.

Practice zero-based thinking in all your marketing efforts. Ask the question, "Is there anything that I am doing today that, knowing what I now know, I wouldn't start up again today if I had to do it over?"

Is there any product or service that you would not bring to the market today, knowing what you now know? Is there any marketing or sales activity that you would not begin again today, knowing what you now know? Is there any business process that you are engaged in that, knowing what you now know, you would not start up again today if you had to do it over?

By asking this question on a regular basis, you continue to clear your mind and open yourself up to new possibilities. It is amazing and unfortunate how many companies are locked into doing things that, knowing what they now know, they would never start up again and that require unnecessary time and expense. Remaining locked in the old and unworkable detracts from the energy that you need to develop new products and services, and new ways of marketing them, that are more appropriate for the market of today.

Keep Your Mind Open

Be creative. Resist the comfort zone. Refuse to follow the path of least resistance, continuing to do what you have always done in the past. Look for newer, better, faster, cheaper, easier, more convenient, and less expensive ways of marketing and selling your products and services. Be open to the possibility that anything or everything that you are doing today will soon be rendered obsolete by changing markets and aggressive competition. Be open to change, and when you get an idea, move quickly before someone else does.

As Satchel Paige, the baseball player, once said, "Don't look back. Someone might be gaining on you."

Summary and Conclusion

MARKETING IS the most exciting of all business sports. It is the heartbeat of every successful business. It is continually changing in response to the explosion of information, the expansion of technology, and the aggressiveness of competition, at all levels and everywhere.

All business strategy is marketing strategy. Your ability to think clearly and well about the very best marketing strategies, and to continually change and upgrade your activities, is the key to the future of your business.

Fortunately, like all business skills, marketing can be learned by practice, experimentation, and continually making mistakes. The key is to test, test, test. And whatever marketing strategy is working for you today, no matter how successful it is, will soon be obsolete and will have to be replaced by a new or different market strategy.

Your competition determines your sales, market share, and profitability. And your competition has never been more determined and more aggressive than it is today. Your job is to be better, faster, and more creative than your competitors, continually leapfrogging them in the marketplace to attain market leadership. Fortunately, there are no limits on what you can accomplish, except for the limits that you place on yourself.

Good luck!

ABOUT THE AUTHOR

Brian Tracy is a professional speaker, trainer, seminar leader, and consultant, and chairman of Brian Tracy International, a training and consulting company based in Solana Beach, California.

Brian bootstrapped his way to success. In 1981, in talks and seminars around the U.S., he began teaching the principles he forged in sales and business. Today, his books and audio and video programs—more than 500 of them—are available in 38 languages and are used in 55 countries.

He is the bestselling author of more than fifty books, including *Full Engagement* and *Reinvention*.

"Inspiring, entertaining, informative, motivational..."
Brian Tracy is one of the world's top speakers. He addresses more than 250,000 people annually—in over 100 appearances—and has consulted and trained at more than 1,000 corporations. In his career he has reached over five million people in 58 countries. He has lived and practiced every principle in his writing and speeches:

21st-Century Thinking: How to outmaneuver the competition and get superior results in an ever-turbulent business climate.

Leadership in the New Millennium: Learn the most powerful leadership principles—ever—to get maximum results, faster.

Advanced Selling Strategies: How to use modern sales' most advanced strategies and tactics to outperform your competitors.

The Psychology of Success: Think and act like the top performers. Learn practical, proven techniques for excellence.

To book Brian to speak at your next meeting or conference, visit Brian Tracy International at www.briantracy.com, or call (858) 436-7316 for a free promotional package. Brian will carefully customize his talk to your specific needs.